CHINESE ZODIAC

T&J

Published by TAJ Books International LLC 2014
5501 Kincross Lane
Charlotte, North Carolina, USA
28277

www.tajbooks.com
www.tajminibooks.com

All notations of errors or omissions (author inquiries, permissions) concerning the content of this book should be addressed to info@tajbooks.com. The publisher wishes to thank Cristiano Del Riccio, Paul Bird, Eva Rinaldi, Petr Novák (Wikipedia), Jakub Hałun, Rob Bogaerts/Anefo, Ian Smith, Christopher Peterson, Gage Skidmore, Allan Warren, Towpilot, Nicolas Genin, Romain Dubois, and Miuki.

ISBN 978-1-84406-246-1

Printed in China
1 2 3 4 5 18 17 16 15 14

CHINESE ZODIAC

鼠 牛 虎
兔 龍 蛇
馬 羊 猴
雞 狗 豬

T&J

BY ISABELLA ALSTON AND
KATHRYN DIXON

CHINESE ZODIAC

The majority of the Western world associates astrology with those four- or five-lined daily horoscopes that often pop up regularly in the pages of magazines, newspapers, and of course on the Internet. Even if you are not a strong believer in the pithy prognostications of astrologers, you may still read your horoscope out of amusement or sheer curiosity, but then think little to nothing of it for the rest of the day or month.

The short, bare-bones astrological horoscope that the average person comes in contact with barely begins to skim the surface of what astrology truly is, however. First, the popularized horoscopes refer to only one form of astrology: what we now call Western astrology. This form of astrology was developed centuries ago by the Babylonians in an attempt to plot the constant movements of the celestial heavens and phases of the moon in order to understand and disseminate the best times to plant and harvest crops. Over time, these methods of celestial mapping organically developed into a complicated system of divination based on the positions of the planets. Simultaneously, in the Far East, the Chinese were busy doing just what the Babylonians were doing, although in a slightly different way.

The origins of Chinese astrology can be traced to the Han Dynasty (stretching from the second century BC to the AD second century) and evolved in close association to broad Chinese philosophical concepts, most notably Confucianism and Taoism. These philosophies seek to explore, understand, and explain the world in a way that unifies the mind and spirit. The system of astrology that developed in the East was consistent with the prevailing religious or spiritual beliefs of the population, which were primarily polytheistic and mythologically based. The primary Eastern religions of Buddhism, Hinduism, Shinto, Taoism, Confucianism, Jainism, and Sikhism remain indelibly linked with Eastern cultures today. The more abstract or esoteric nature of astrology does not present the conflicts in the East that it inevitably does in the West.

Yin–Yang symbol surrounded by Chinese characters for each of the twelve Chinese zodiac signs

CHINESE ZODIAC

The Eastern experience contrasts sharply with the Western experience of astrology. The differences between Western astrological principles and Judeo-Christian beliefs may explain why today the Chinese zodiac is more openly accepted in Eastern culture than Western astrology is accepted in Western culture. In other words, Western culture has largely adopted monotheistic religions and has widely embraced science and Western medicine to a much greater degree over the years than their Eastern brethren. Both science and Western medicine challenge the basic principles of astrology.

The main premise of Chinese astrology is based on the concept of *Wu Xing*: a complex explanation of life determined by five phases or energies derived from the five elements of wood, fire, earth, metal, and water and the multitude of interactions and relationships that exist among them. In order to understand just exactly what *Wu Xing* means, it helps to understand that the term itself is still to this day incapable of being translated directly into English. The most generally accepted translation by modern sinologists of *Wu Xing* is that of "changing states of being." Other translations such as "permutations" and "metamorphoses of being" are similar enough to the former that one could conclude *Wu Xing* stands for the continually changing and evolving nature of all elements of life, neatly collapsed into the five basic earthly elements.

Furthermore, the Chinese character, *Wu*, translates literally into "no" while *Xing* translates literally into "type" or "mold," so a direct English translation at its most basic of "no type" or "no mold" could be the best way to fully understand what is rather abstract terminology. It also helps to compare the Western world's understanding of the earthly elements to the Eastern world's concept. In the West, the elements are understood to be the basic building blocks of matter. In the East, the elements are viewed much less concretely and instead are believed to be ever-changing and constantly morphing elements or energies. These energies are what compose life on earth, although they are not perceived of as existing in a physical form.

The Jade Emperor, who according to Chinese folk culture is the ruler of Heaven and all realms of existence below, including the worlds of Man and Hell, selecting the twelve animals represented in the Chinese zodiac

The Forbidden City in Beijing was the home of the Chinese emperor during the Ming Dynasty (1368–1644) and the Qing Dynasty (1644–1912), as depicted in a Ming Dynasty painting

The basic concept of *Wu Xing*, which gave birth to Chinese astrology, began to take shape around AD 500 in China and was passed down through the years in the form of oral tradition. The Chinese ancient philosophical text, the *I Ching* (*Book of Changes*), first recorded the concept of *Wu Xing*. This is the starting point for understanding modern Chinese astrology and where we have solid documentation explaining these concepts. Chinese astrology holds that each individual is born with two different sides to their personality: *xian tian* and *hou tian*.

The first, *xian tian*, is a person's core make-up or temperament. *Xian tian* is inherent in the being as an individual and remains so for the entirety of life on this planet. The second, *hou tian*, is the part of the personality that is acquired and developed on throughout life and is affected not just by who you "are," but also by your surroundings, circumstances, and experiences. The combination of these two "faces" of an individual determines overall character.

Another important aspect of Chinese astrology is fate and the idea that everyone is born with a set fate in life and a reason for their existence. This belief is referred to as *ming yun* and is related to the concept of reincarnation, that is, after death the soul, or most basic spiritual form of an individual, when not tied to the earthly body, carries with it past life experiences and lessons that were either learned or need to be learned. Thus, an individual's current life reflects all past lives and thus directly affects the individual's fate in this life.

Tian ming, which is translated as our "daily lot in life," deals with destiny rather than fate. In order to achieve *tian ming*, an individual must be able to harmonize spirit and soul. Lastly, fate is of three types known as "Heaven luck," "Man luck," and "Earth luck." The first form, Heaven luck, is the broadest of the three and refers to what can be best described as the spiritual guide to life. The second, or Man luck, is fate that can be controlled by day-to-day choices and actions. The last, Earth luck, addresses how we control our physical surroundings and is thus tied into the practice and concept of *feng shui*.

CHINESE ZODIAC

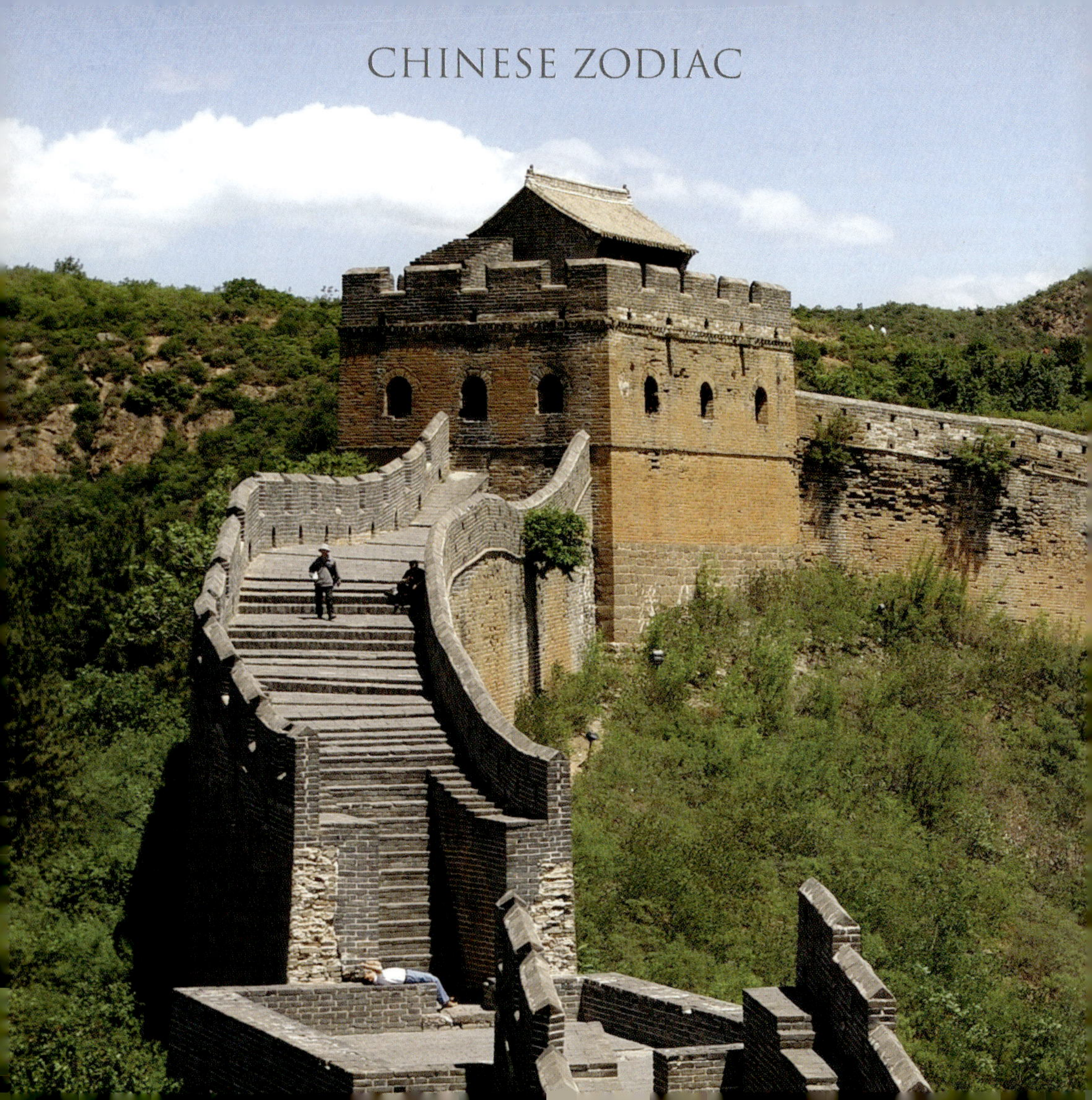

A section of the Great Wall of China near Jinshanling

CHINESE ZODIAC

THE FIVE ELEMENTS

WOOD

FIRE

EARTH

METAL

WATER

Ancient Chinese wisdom sought to express the delicate balance between the forces of Heaven and Earth that they believed ruled all aspects of life and of living beings. Astutely, the Chinese masters described *Qi* (pronounced "chee") as the life force, or soul, having an energy that flows almost seamlessly from positive to negative, masculine to feminine, aggressive to passive, night/dark to day/light, fiery to watery, receiving to giving, respectively, as symbolized by the Yin–Yang. Each of the animal signs in the Chinese zodiac embodies this concept of energy, *Qi*, and of the balance between the two aspects or opposites of the energy force. Because of where each sign falls within the sixty-year cycle of the Chinese zodiac, each sign is influenced uniquely by the five elements, the ten Heavenly Stems, and the twelve Earthly Branches. These influences distinguish each of the signs from the others and thus the personalities exhibited by those who are born under the signs.

What began as an attempt of mankind nearly 4,000 years ago to understand the seasons and to improve the farmers' harvests, gradually evolved into a system that could be employed to determine auspicious dates regarding matters of importance to the Chinese emperors. Eventually, the practice began to incorporate the divining of the fortunes of the emperors, and over time the practice spread to the wider Chinese population. By the time of the T'ang Dynasty (AD 618–907), the idea of fortune-telling was so popular that an encyclopedia was written for this purpose. Chinese astrology holds an important place in the daily lives of many citizens of Eastern nations today.

CHINESE ZODIAC

THE JADE EMPEROR

Chinese folk lore attributes the specific selection of the animals in the Chinese zodiac to the Jade Emperor who ruled the heavens, earth, and hell. Because he dwelled in Heaven, he had never encountered any of the animals that lived on the earth. He was quite curious about their appearance, what sounds they made, and how they spent their days and nights. Did they contribute to the world around them? Were they helpful to mankind?

Thousands of animals roamed the land, flew above in the air, and swam in the seas and streams. Because there were too many to invite to visit him in Heaven, he asked his advisors to select a dozen that would be the most important for him to meet. But which to choose? The emperor's advisor began by inviting his friend the rat who in turn asked his friend the cat. The cat, thrilled to be included, asked the rat to wake him so he would not be late. The rat, worried that the cat was much more beautiful than he, decided not to wake the cat.

The following morning all of the invited animals except the cat appeared for review before the Jade Emperor. Puzzled as to why only eleven animals were there to meet the emperor, the advisor quickly sent a servant to Earth to find a twelfth animal. The first animal he saw was a pig in a farmer's arms. Hastily, the servant grabbed the pig and returned to Heaven to present the pig to the Jade Emperor.

The rat, whose hopes of impressing the Jade Emperor burned brightly in his mind, jumped on the ox's back and began to play the flute. The rat achieved the attention he so desperately craved, enchanting the Emperor who granted him the first place among the twelve animals. The ox was awarded the second place because of his generosity toward the rat. Each of the other animals was deliberately chosen for their rank within the group: the tiger was courageous so was placed third, all the way to the last animal, the pig, because he arrived, well, last.

At the very end of the animals' visit with the Jade Emperor, the cat came bounding into the palace where he realized that he was soundly duped by his friend the rat. Seeing the rat, the cat gave chase and that is why cats hunt rats (and mice) to this day.

THE TWELVE ANIMAL SIGNS AND THE SIXTY-YEAR CYCLE

Chinese time is measured in a sixty-year cycle. Each year represents one of the twelve animals, and each animal transitions through the influence of each of the five elements: earth, fire, water, metal, and wood. Symbolizing the interaction of Heaven and Earth are the influences of the ten Heavenly Stems and twelve Earthly Branches. In addition, a number of other factors bring yet other layers of influence to a unique horoscope.

Each Earthly Branch is associated with one of the twelve animals of the zodiac as well as a season and a compass direction. Each of the Heavenly Stems is associated with one of the five elements. The sixty-year cycle always begins with *Chia Tzu* (Wood Rat) and ends with *Kuei Hai* (Water Pig). Until 1912 when China became a republic and was no longer a dynastic empire, the Chinese calendar used the sixty-year system. Surely, the centuries-old tradition of a sixty-year cycle governing the most basic function of life–time–is difficult to ignore in the modern age even after the passage of an entire century. The continual repetition of a sixty-year time cycle also interestingly highlights the basic, unchanging nature of mankind and his impact on the world around him. The saying "The more things change, the more they stay the same" impresses upon us a similar meaning.

The current sixty-year cycle began in 1984.

CHINESE ZODIAC

Hour	Earthly Branch	Animal	Characteristics of Person Born in Hour
11pm-1am	Tzu	Rat	Hot-tempered, impulsive, but can learn with age. Works best alone.
1am-3am	Ch'ou	Ox	Career may be a challenge in youth, but improves with age. Seek your fortune far from home.
3am-5am	Yin	Tiger	Youthful years may see family problems, but these improve as time passes.
5am-7am	Mao	Rabbit	Parents are very supportive. Sun shines on you as a child. Romance is problematic until mid-age.
7am-9am	Ch'en	Dragon	Positive outlook on life. Strong friendships keep your life busy. Optimism sees you through.
9am-11am	Szu	Snake	Successful in business and financial matters. Tempted by luxury. Generous with family.
11am-1pm	Wu	Horse	You must learn to compromise early in life. Change can be difficult. Beware the mundane.
1pm-3pm	Wei	Goat	A curious nature leads to fickleness in career. Troubled family and romantic life when young.
3pm-5pm	Shen	Monkey	Generally lucky, especially in money matters. Big spender. Balance romantic and career pursuits.
5pm-7pm	Yu	Rooster	Fame may beckon from afar but family will always be in your heart. Friendships form easily.
7pm-9pm	Hsu	Dog	Works well alone as is very capable. Looks on the bright side and enjoys variety and opportunity.
9pm-11pm	Hai	Pig	Hard-working and handy, you have many talents. You are not a half-way person.

Each day in the Chinese calendar is divided into twelve "hours." Each of the hours corresponds to two hours in the Western calendar. The time a person is born falls within one of these hours. Certain characteristics are identified with each of the twelve hours. The chart to the left explains the meaning of the birth hour.

Like the hour of birth, the day of birth also influences the traits of each person. The chart below explains the meaning of the birth day.

Days	Characteristics of Person Born on Day
1st, 10th, 19th, 28th	You are defined by the high standards you set for yourself but can sometimes disregard the needs of others in your quest to achieve them.
2nd, 11th, 20th, 29th	Fun-loving and gregarious, you are popular, but also seek solitude and quiet. You can be quick tempered if under pressure.
3rd, 12th, 21st, 30th	Your hard-working nature makes you an astute business person. You are very competitive and may be off-putting to those who do not know you.
4th, 13th, 22nd, 31st	Somewhat reticent and quiet, people may see you as cold and aloof. Your patience lends itself to a career in academics.
5th, 14th, 23rd	You are clever but have a fiery temperament. Because you have difficulty seeing others' points of view, you may miss your golden opportunity.
6th, 15th, 24th	Often you live with your head in the clouds, which may hamper your ability to prosper. You attract people with your open nature. An artistic career is often your path.
7th, 16th, 25th	Travel, intrigue, and adventure are your siren call. Be careful to keep your head on straight and make an effort to be self-disciplined.
8th, 17th, 26th	Observant and reflective, you are happiness when working alone. You are a bit of a gypsy, meeting both fortune and hardship on your life journey.
9th, 18th, 27th	Greeting the world with open arms you have many friends. Moodiness can invade your happy nature, however, and upset those who are close to you.

THE LUNAR CALENDAR

For many readings in Chinese astrology it is necessary to know the lunar equivalent of the Western solar date. The phases of the moon form the basis of the lunar calendar in contrast to the solar calendar, which is based on the movements of the sun. The lunar year has twelve moons representing a lunar month. Each moon has 29½ days so that a complete year of twelve moons fall short of the solar year of 365 days by eleven days. Typically, six of the lunar months are "small" months of 29 days and six are "large" months equal to 30 days, but depending on the year, either can expand to seven months. In order to adjust the lunar calendar to the solar calendar, approximately every three years an extra month is added to the lunar calendar.

Unfortunately, it is beyond the scope of this book to provide the necessary grid to translate your solar calendar dates to your lunar calendar dates. That information is easily located on the Internet, however, so seek it out if you wish to learn even more about what Chinese astrology says about you!

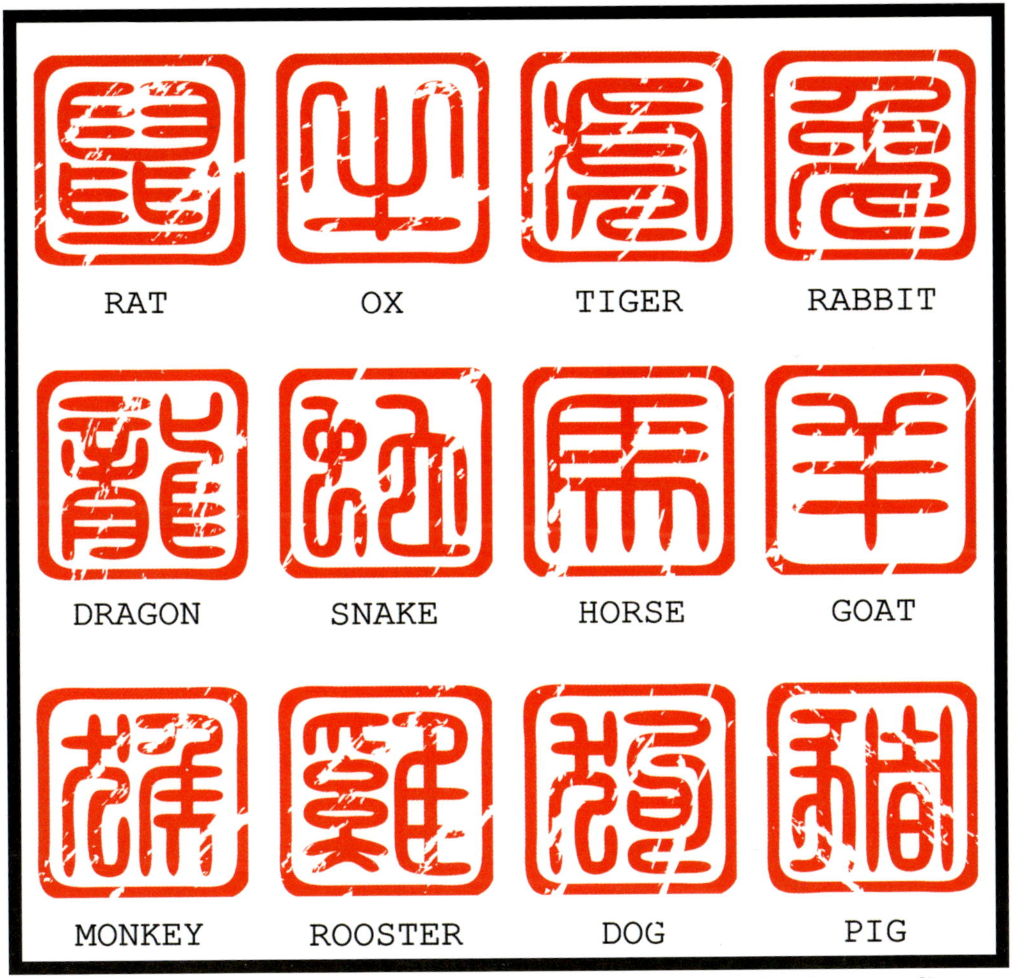

Chinese character for each of the twelve animal signs of the Chinese zodiac

YEAR OF THE RAT

12 February 1888–30 January 1889	Earth Rat
31 January 1900–08 February 1901	Metal Rat
18 February 1912–05 February 1913	Water Rat
05 February 1924–23 January 1925	Wood Rat
24 January 1936–10 February 1937	Fire Rat
10 February 1948–28 January 1949	Earth Rat
28 January 1960–14 February 1961	Metal Rat
15 February 1972–02 February 1973	Water Rat
02 February 1984–19 February 1985	Wood Rat
19 February 1996–06 February 1997	Fire Rat
07 February 2008–25 January 2009	Earth Rat
25 January 2020–11 February 2021	Metal Rat

Rat people are charming and expressive. They like people and are comfortable in social situations as well as in one-on-one conversations. Rats are typically gregarious and rarely spend time alone. Perhaps this trait hides an unwillingness to open up to others. The majority of Rat people tend to have more acquaintances than true friends leading to rather shallow relationships. When deep friendships do blossom, however, the Rat is a friend for life, in thick and thin, in good times and bad.

Reluctant to confide in others, Rats contribute to keeping people at arm's distance. Their talkativeness and gregariousness more often than not hides this trait and those around them are unaware of what the Rat is holding close to the vest.

Rat people can be narrow minded, but are unfailingly honest. The Rat has a quick wit with which he keeps his head above water, typically making a good living. The Rat is without doubt a perfectionist who is critical of others, making Rat people a difficult work partner, colleague, or boss. Watch out! Confidence, exacerbated by stubbornness, marks the steely manner of the Rat.

YEAR OF THE RAT

These characteristics of hard-working, hard-charging Rats are complemented by fantastic organization skills, charisma, and outstanding socio-personal behaviors. The Rat has what it takes to be a good businessman or politician. Hard-earned money slips through her fingers as quickly as she makes it though which may explain why the Rat is not financially generous with her friends. Restless and often looking for the next big break, Rats can get impatient for power and money, leading some to struggle the desire to gamble and with the destructive consequences of such pursuits.

The Rat is not romantic, but he is sensual, loving, and passionate, and unabashedly loyal and devoted to his family.

Being ranked first in the Chinese astrological chart, Rats are generally pioneers and at the forefront of the action, translating at times into a self-aggrandizing self-assessment. Rats tend to lead busy lives and enjoy living dangerously, however with their formidable problem solving ability are able to extricate themselves just in the nick of time. They make for an exhausting travel companion and will speed off to the distant corners of the world at a moment's notice.

Rats generally present a cool facade to the outside world, regardless of their inner feelings. Passion in many forms roils deep within their hearts and minds and souls. An inability to discuss their feelings freely with those they love can generate angst and aggravation for all concerned. Emotional repression by the Rat can lead to a continuous cycle of unhappiness with life's circumstances and with friends and family.

An emotional roller-coaster is often the experience of Rats in love. Rats seek security in amorous relationships. Their charm does not typically mean game playing with their partner. When security is achieved the Rat's charm is focused full force on the loved one. But if that security is ever shaken, the Rat often resonds with secretiveness, restiveness, and deflection.

Auspicious careers: Salesperson, art or film critic, politician, writer

YEAR OF THE RAT

ELEMENT
Yang Water

SEASON
Winter

MONTH
December

HOUR
23:00–01:00

FENG SHUI DIRECTION
North

RANK
First

WESTERN SIGN
Sagittarius

FRAGRANCE
Sandalwood

FLOWER
Holly

FAMOUS RATS

William Shakespeare

Antonio Banderas

Prince Charles

Gwyneth Paltrow

Vanessa Redgrave

George Washington

YEAR OF THE RAT

Compatability of the Rat with the other zodiac signs:

Rat and Rat–Intensely passionate; very like-minded, but such similarity may grow old and lose its charm. The two friends or couple share a rich sense of humor and joviality. A positive outlook is also shared by both, so that any problems in the friendship or love can typically be resolved if both parties so wish.

Rat and Ox–Mutually respectful; naturally complementary in temperament with the Rat seeking new opportunity and the Ox offering wise advice. The spontaneity of the Rat can jostle the staid Ox off his tried-and-true rutted road.

Rat and Tiger–Willingly adventurous; both signs welcome the challenges presented by change, frequently bored by everyday life. The Rat's fear and insecurity can be balanced by the Tiger's welcoming of the world with open arms and hefting the Rat upon his shoulder.

Rat and Rabbit–Jointly seeking security and comfort; nevertheless the two signs approach the search from conflicting perspectives: the Rat with nervous energy and the Rabbit with peaceful reflection. The two are often in conflict.

Rat and Dragon–Socially compatible; both signs hold their own with an audience and both feed off of the other's energy. They do not stand in each other's way.

Rat and Snake–Keenly attuned; passion abounds between these two signs. The Snake is easily tempted by the fruit of another, of course, and if the Rat gets wind of an indiscretion, the Rat's insecurity bubbles up making it difficult to salvage the once exuberant emotional ties.

Rat and Horse–Emotionally charged; the Horse canters wildly through the fields of romance triggering the Rat's innate wariness to go to ground. The Horse can suffer the critical eye of the Rat, severing their previously uninhibited relationship.

Rat and Goat–Determinedly different; these two signs must find common ground to build a friendship or partnership. The Rat forges ahead while the Goat hangs back to chew his cud.

Rat and Monkey–Highly competitive; the intellectual and sensual high-wire act of the Monkey is not to be outdone by the overwhelming intensity and passion of the Rat. But when the two energies collide, one or both suffers the fall.

Rat and Rooster–Initially at odds; opposites attract but it make take some time before these two signs recognize their winning combination. At first, in the Rat's eyes the Rooster may appear superficial and frivolous, but perseverence tells the tale. The Rooster's courage and analytical nature will win over the critical Rat.

Rat and Dog–Fearlessly supportive; trustworthy Dog and watchful Rat can forge a life-long bond.

Rat and Pig–Happily affectionate; innocent and cheerful Pig takes Rat's demanding nature in stride. Pig's compassion assuages Rat's perception that she is misunderstood.

YEAR OF THE OX

31 January 1889–20 January 1890	Earth Ox
19 February 1901–07 February 1902	Metal Ox
06 February 1913–25 January 1914	Water Ox
24 January 1925–12 February 1926	Wood Ox
11 February 1937–30 January 1938	Fire Ox
29 January 1949–16 February 1950	Earth Ox
15 February 1961–04 February 1962	Metal Ox
03 February 1973–22 January 1974	Water Ox
20 February 1985–08 February 1986	Wood Ox
07 February 1997–27 January 1998	Fire Ox
26 January 2009–13 February 2010	Earth Ox
12 February 2021–31 January 2022	Metal Ox

Ox people, just like the mighty Ox that characterizes them, are hard working and persistent. They stick to the problem or task at hand and don't easily give up. Black and white is the way they see the world. Their high standards, although morally and ethically rewarding for themselves, are often used to fairly or not judge those who fall short of these ideals.

Ox people are not fond of social occasions and do not seek the limelight. They remain quiet in a crowd. Like its namesake, the Ox can cause a ruckus when enraged. Large and muscular, Oxens storm the premises and anyone in their way, impulsive and frightening when angry. Beware the emotionally hurt or demoralized Ox!

Yet the more commonly quiet and tranquil Ox is observing his surroundings all the time. The Ox's memory puts that of elephants to shame, and they will happily relate their observations to you with great deliberation and detail. Those details are often put to good use in their profession when attention to detail and observation are paramount.

YEAR OF THE OX

Like the Ox who digs in his heels and will not budge, Ox people are stubborn in their beliefs and are proud to stand by them. And they stand by their friends and family members just as staunchly as they uphold their personal standards and beliefs. Patience is also a trait of the Ox, making them a fast and true life-long friend. Seldom jealous, they will, however, expect the unfailing loyalty and fidelity of their spouse. Traditionalists, they are very family oriented and conservative. Self-sacrifice is a common trait. People born under the influence of the Ox are kind and caring. They are logical, with a great deal of common sense. Achieving financial and relationship security occupies their thoughts and drives their energies. They do not shrink from hard work because they know it will bring them what they seek for themselves and their families. Strong-minded and individualistic, most Oxen are independent and self-reliant.

The Ox is methodical, approaching work with intelligence, reflection, and tenacity. Ox people like to lead in both professional and personal relationships. They do not shy away from responsibility. Although the Ox's strength inspires confidence, it can also be perceived as rigidity, obstinacy, and ponderousness.

Inspiring and teaching others by example is an everyday event for Ox people whose dedication to their high standards is simply a way of life. Respect for others and a conscientious attitude toward their place in the world makes them outstanding citizens.

Oxen make solid, reliable partners who are tender and devoted but rarely romantic. Their affection is genuine for those they cherish, but they are cool and distant to anyone with whom they are not intimate, physically or emotionally. Getting close to an Ox is a challenge. Once a commitment is made, however, the Ox is a loyal friend and partner, rarely straying in search of greener pastures.

Auspicious careers: surgeon, craftsman, veterinarian, architect

YEAR OF THE OX

ELEMENT
Yin Earth

SEASON
Winter

MONTH
January

HOUR
1:00–03:00

FENG SHUI DIRECTION
North Northeast

RANK
Second

WESTERN SIGN
Capricorn

FRAGRANCE
Frankincense

FLOWER
Carnation

FAMOUS OXEN

Sammy Davis, Jr.

Margaret Thatcher

Napoleon Bonaparte

Adolf Hitler

George Clooney

YEAR OF THE OX

Compatability of the Ox with the other zodiac signs:

Ox and Rat—Mutually respectful; naturally complementary in temperament with the Rat seeking new opportunity and the Ox offering wise advice. The spontaneity of the Rat can jostle the staid Ox off his tried-and-true rutted road.

Ox and Ox—Well-organized; cut from the same cloth, these Oxen are steady and reliable in work and friendship. They agree on the wisdom of the idiom: Act in haste, repent at leisure. Sometimes, however, a double dose of cautiousness becomes tedious and spontaneity is the cure.

Ox and Tiger—Oddly at odds; a bit of push and pull between these two signs can keep the fires burning, but it can also wreak havoc. Rambunctious Tiger can keep staid Ox happy, but flirtatious Tiger can push insecure Ox into retreat.

Ox and Rabbit—Contentedly nonconfrontational; happy to enjoy the mundane, the Ox and the Rabbit appreciate their lot in life and what the other brings to it. The Rabbit is the jumpier of the two and the Ox's stability soothes the Rabbit.

Ox and Dragon—Attractively opposite; the enthusiastic, charismatic Dragon wows the dependable, strong-willed Ox until the two wills clash. Finding a happy compromise is essential for a long-term relationship.

Ox and Snake—Positively partners; a deep karmic understanding exists between these two signs. The charming Snake is happy to venture into the world to make the couple's fortune and the steadfast Ox is content to keep the home fires burning.

YEAR OF THE OX

Ox and Horse—Poorly suited; these two four-hooved signs march to different drummers. Restless and flighty, the Horse bounds away to discover new adventures, while the Ox, patient and supporting, watches in disappointment.

Ox and Goat—Decidedly dissimilar; opposite approaches to life mean unbridled consternation in partnership. Sensible, organized Ox does not see eye to eye with fanciful Goat, but Goat's good intentions can melt away Ox's distain.

Ox and Monkey—Slowly trusting; with time these two signs gradually learn to appreciate the other's traits that balance their own. Chattering Monkey stays busy, only to return home to responsible Ox. Nevertheless, Ox can grow tired of Monkey's vivacity and gregariousness.

Ox and Rooster—Delightfully happy; the perfect blend of fun and respect weaves the fabric of a long-lasting relationship. The Rooster brings the color and design whereas the Ox brings the patience and tenacity. Stay clear of the sparks these two generate!

Ox and Dog—Unerring fealty; the loyal natures of both signs seal their hearts and minds for the long haul. Fretting Dog is soothed by reliable Ox enabling the partners to meet life's challenges head on, even in times of pain and sorrow.

Ox and Pig—Soulfully suited; old-fashioned values keep these two cosily at home most nights, but when playful Pig persuades parsimonious Ox to spring for a night on the town, both appreciate the gift the other brings their relationship.

YEAR OF THE TIGER

08 February 1902–28 January 1903	Water Tiger
26 January 1914–13 February 1915	Wood Tiger
13 February 1926–01 February 1927	Fire Tiger
31 January 1938–18 February 1939	Earth Tiger
17 February 1950–05 February 1951	Metal Tiger
05 February 1962–24 January 1963	Water Tiger
23 January 1974–10 February 1975	Wood Tiger
09 February 1986–28 January 1987	Fire Tiger
28 January 1998–15 February 1999	Earth Tiger
14 February 2010–02 February 2011	Metal Tiger
01 February 2022-21 January 2023	Water Tiger

Tigers are born leaders, noble and fearless, respected for their courage, even by their enemies, which inevitably surface as Tigers pace and protect their turf. Everyone in the Tiger's path appreciates this person of immense power and strength. Unremittingly intense, dynamic, and independent, Tiger people attract many admirers along with their enemies.

Unpredictable by nature, Tigers will surprise with unfettered generosity, even if just after fighting a stiff battle over some selfish matter. The Tiger is a study in contrasts: warm and loving one minute and ferocious and heartless the next. But they are born humanitarians. Injustice angers them like no other wrong.

Second only to the king of the jungle, the lion, Tigers are very confident in their abilities, sometimes verging on overconfidence, which can get them into trouble.

Adventure is the Tiger's mantra. The magnetic personality of Tiger people is difficult to resist and their innate air of authority and natural leadership confers upon them a certain prestige. All Tigers love the spotlight. It is their destiny.

Tigers are moved by a sense of urgency and usually operate alone. They are not intimated by hard work. A task assigned to a Tiger will be undertaken and accomplished with enthusiasm and efficiency. Although Tigers are capable of earning a very good wage, they are not interested in money as a solitary goal, but typically money finds them, even if they do not seek it.

Sensitive and emotional, Tigers love tenderly, but can become dangerously intense. Possessiveness can be a problem for those who share their lives. Compounding this tendency is the desire for a nontraditional life, challenging the expectations of many a spouse.

Their kindness, honesty, and charm work in their favor to smooth potential conflicts with friends and family. Many a Tiger lives a solitary life, if not in terms of friends and family, in terms of his or her state of mind in pursuing daily and future goals. The Tiger slips quietly alone through the jungle in search of his quarry, fearing no-one and seeking help from no-one.

Travel and adventure tempt the Tiger. Exotic locales beckon to energetic, curious Tiger people. Tiger parents are excellent role models for their children in such situations, encouraging them to push boundaries and observe the world around them, often happening upon the downtrodden and weak to which they offer solace and support. What child wouldn't benefit from such an experience?

Auspicious careers: chief executive, military officer, performer, mercenary

YEAR OF THE TIGER

ELEMENT
Yang Wood

SEASON
Spring

MONTH
February

HOUR
03:00–05:00

FENG SHUI DIRECTION
North

RANK
Third

WESTERN SIGN
Aquarius

FRAGRANCE
Citrus

FLOWER
Violet

FAMOUS TIGERS

Dwight Eisenhower

Queen Elizabeth II

Ludwig van Beethoven

Oscar Wilde

Paula Abdul

Natalie Wood

YEAR OF THE TIGER

Compatability of the Tiger with the other zodiac signs:

Tiger and Rat–Willingly adventurous; both signs welcome the challenges presented by change, frequently bored by everyday life. The Rat's fear and insecurity can be balanced by the Tiger's welcoming of the world with open arms and hefting the Rat upon his shoulder.

Tiger and Ox–Oddly at odds; a bit of push and pull between these two signs can keep the fires burning, but it can also wreak havoc. Rambunctious Tiger can keep staid Ox happy, but flirtatious Tiger can push insecure Ox into retreat.

Tiger and Tiger–Domestically disorganized; the combination of these two wild beasts can only be described as the clash of the titans! Two independent natures that seek excitement at every turn, often in opposing directions, can make for some topsy-turvy days and nights. Give each other room to roam and you'll be happy.

Tiger and Rabbit–Quietly intimate; the Tiger is a natural wanderer but shares with Rabbit the desire for security at home. Insert versatility and variation among the routine affairs of daily life and both will be content. Quiet moments at home will arrest Rabbit's fears when Tiger gets restless.

Tiger and Dragon–Passionately unpredictable; with two signs so characterized by extreme energy and enthusiasm for living, the possibilities are endless. High spirits and strong opinions will inevitably cause disagreements, but the joy of sharing life's journey will prevail.

Tiger and Snake–Irritatingly antagonistic; if ever two signs approach life in different ways, it's these two. The Tiger is action incarnate, while the Snake prefers strategy and analysis. Whether in matters of finance, romance or simply making dinner, if the two signs compromise and negotiate, they can be very happy.

Tiger and Horse–Enthusiastically social; a shared passion for life and the people in it bind these two signs together. A very hectic social calendar makes for a chaotic home life.

Tiger and Goat–Reassuringly protective; the Tiger is eager to guard the Goat against unwanted confrontations and demands. Both signs are independent in their own ways and neither wishes to feel trapped in a relationship.

Tiger and Monkey–Energetically adventurous; both the Tiger and the Monkey literally jump at any new opportunity for exploration and new experiences, but the Monkey thinks before jumping and is usually the one to resolve obstacles.

Tiger and Rooster–Critically frank; neither sign hesitates to speak its mind. Be patient with the other's censure and be honest about your own feelings.

Tiger and Dog–Keenly compassionate; these signs work well together to fight for those less fortunate.

Tiger and Pig–Unbounded friendship; balancing each sign's needs for companionship and freedom is the key to mutual happiness. The Pig listens to the advice of the Tiger, and the Tiger responds to the admonitions of the Pig.

YEAR OF THE RABBIT

09 February 1891-29 January 1892	Metal Rabbit
29 January 1903–15 February 1904	Water Rabbit
14 February 1915–02 February 1916	Wood Rabbit
02 February 1927–22 January 1928	Fire Rabbit
19 February 1939–07 February 1940	Earth Rabbit
06 February 1951–26 January 1952	Metal Rabbit
25 January 1963–12 February 1964	Water Rabbit
11 February 1975–30 January 1976	Wood Rabbit
29 January 1987–16 February 1988	Fire Rabbit
16 February 1999–04 February 2000	Earth Rabbit
03 February 2011–22 January 2012	Metal Rabbit
22 January 2023–09 February 2024	Water Rabbit

Rabbit people seek freedom from the chaotic and hectic world around them, creating comfort and privacy in their home surroundings. Most have relatively calm temperaments, but when their peace and tranquility is threatened they can virtually disappear without a word in an effort to regain their inner centeredness.

Typically, Rabbits are intuitive and prefer to listen to their inner voice rather than take advice from friends or family. If you ever lose a Rabbit, take a wander along a secluded garden path or a peek inside a shady arbor. The Rabbit always has a safe, inviting warren nearby in which to escape the pressures of the mundane.

The emotionally balanced Rabbit is persuasive, compassionate, diplomatic, and discerning, but when emotions are not balanced the Rabbit can be aloof, secretive, and easily offended by others. Sensitive Rabbit is attuned to the energies of most personal and professional circumstances, quickly analyzing the situation in light of his or her best interests and assessing expedient options.

YEAR OF THE RABBIT

Most Rabbits are capable of remaining calm in emergencies and dislike drama in every instance. Somewhat surprisingly, however, a Rabbit can become the life of the party, but only after mental, emotional, and pyschological energies have been replenished from rest and solitude. Rabbits get along with almost all people because they are adaptable, affable, and sensitive. Conflict and confrontation are not popular with the Rabbit. In such environments, the Rabbit is sure to "go to ground" to avoid them.

Romantic partners can feel confident in the Rabbit's desire to stay close to home. The Rabbit is loyal, but can be easily hurt by a partner's thoughtless or angry remark. In such cases, because the Rabbit's desire for tenderness and security are compromised, he or she withdraws until the problem is resolved.

Although Rabbit people love their families, they are not as family centered as other signs. The same quest for calm and quiet that impacts life outside of family is brought to bear inside the family. The Rabbit parent can appear to be short-tempered due to the frantic demands of children. Things can be quite a different story though after nap time when the Rabbit parent is rejuvenated and the children rested. Then the Rabbit becomes a fun-loving, entertaining parent.

The arts attracts the creative Rabbit as does any career that requires diplomacy. Details make the difference and the Rabbit notices and manages every one. Only when the Rabbit is satisfied that all the candles are lit for a party or all the papers are filed away in the correct folder in the cabinet at work can the Rabbit relax and enjoy his accomplishments.

Auspicious careers: Diplomat, publicist, financial advisor, performer

YEAR OF THE RABBIT

ELEMENT
Yin Wood

SEASON
Spring

MONTH
March

HOUR
05:00–07:00

FENG SHUI DIRECTION
East

RANK
Fourth

WESTERN SIGN
Pisces

FRAGRANCE
Patchouli

FLOWER
Daffodil

FAMOUS RABBITS

Brad Pitt

Jane Seymour

Walt Whitman

Orson Welles

Arthur Miller

Queen Victoria

YEAR OF THE RABBIT

Compatability of the Rabbit with the other zodiac signs:

Rabbit and Rat–Jointly seeking security and comfort; nevertheless the two signs approach the search from conflicting perspectives: the Rat with nervous energy and the Rabbit with peaceful reflection. The two are often in conflict.

Rabbit and Ox–Contentedly nonconfrontational; happy to enjoy the mundane, the Ox and the Rabbit appreciate their lot in life and what the other brings to it. The Rabbit is the jumpier of the two and the Ox's stability soothes the Rabbit.

Rabbit and Tiger–Quietly intimate; the Tiger is a natural wanderer but shares with Rabbit the desire for security at home. Insert versatility and variation among the routine affairs of daily life and both will be content. Quiet moments at home will arrest Rabbit's fears when Tiger gets restless.

Rabbit and Rabbit–Comfortably harmonious; one of a kind, Rabbits are reassureed by burrowing together into a safe and familiar environment. Beauty, both in nature and man-made, enlivens their world. Crisis can upset the Rabbit's apple cart, so being prepared for the unforeseeable is crucial.

Rabbit and Dragon–Sensitively syncopated; the give and take between these two signs helps maintain harmony between them. The extroverted, confident Dragon can threaten the mild-mannered Rabbit's sense of security.

Rabbit and Snake–Simply contemplative; the Rabbit and the Snake share the love of a quiet escape and privacy at home. Their evasion of the hectic world is often in search of beauty: natural as in the outdoors or the genius of man as in a museum or gallery.

Rabbit and Horse—Confidently devoted; romance truly blossoms between these two signs. The Horse's unbridled joy in showing love and tenderness to the Rabbit reassures the Rabbit of the Horse's devotion.

Rabbit and Goat—Truly matched; the world is their oyster and these two signs explore it with abandon! When one is anxious, the other is a calming influence, and vice versa, allowing them to proceed unabated with their adventures.

Rabbit and Monkey—Emotionally intuitive; the clever Monkey's schemes are kept in check by the observant, caring Rabbit who gently guides them both toward a mutual understanding that allows them to grow and learn together.

Rabbit and Rooster—Energetically unbalanced; this is a difficult pairing if emotional equilibrium is the goal. The Rabbit craves harmony and predictability, while the Rooster lives for action and adventure.

Rabbit and Dog—Sensibly realistic; the traits of honor and reliability are shared by these two signs. Both see the world and their place in it the same way, and together can guard against most eventualities that threaten them.

Rabbit and Pig—Naturally harmonious; these signs find it very easy to be together, whether in conversation at home or on a hike through the forest. Listening to each other is the path to achieving their dreams.

YEAR OF THE DRAGON

30 January 1892–16 February 1893	Water Dragon
16 February 1904–03 February 1905	Wood Dragon
03 February 1916–22 January 1917	Fire Dragon
22 January 1928–09 February 1929	Earth Dragon
08 February 1940–26 January 1941	Metal Dragon
27 January 1952–13 February 1953	Water Dragon
13 February 1964–01 February 1965	Wood Dragon
31 January 1976–17 February 1977	Fire Dragon
17 February 1988–05 February 1989	Earth Dragon
05 February 2000–23 January 2001	Metal Dragon
23 January 2012–09 February 2013	Water Dragon

The fodder of fairy tales and medieval lore, the Dragon embodies mystery, power, and ferocity. Dragon people exemplify the very essence of the life force that is symbolized by the fire that burns brightly in their bellies. Characteristically, the Dragon is defiant, aggressive, brave, confident, and ambitious. On the one hand, Dragons make good leaders, and on the other, they can be abhorrent social climbers.

The Dragon is unpredictable, active, shrewd, and influential. Regardless of the situation in which they find themselves, Dragons stand out in a crowd. They are born to be the star quarterback or top salesman. Natural winners, they excel in almost every activity they undertake.

Routine is anathema to them as are obligatory social situations, which they view as unnecessarily tedious. Making matters worse, Dragons always speak their minds and are never short of opinions and beliefs that may be insulting to those around them. They make very disappointing diplomats. Not one to forget a slight, Dragons hold a grudge and are ruthless in its pursuit. If you find yourself on the wrong side of a Dragon, quietly slip into the night until the sparks die out.

That same dedication to a cause is obvious in the Dragon's perfectionistic nature. Never one to give up, the Dragon presses ahead in pursuit of her dreams, many of which are idealistic. Visionaries, prophets, and dreamers are found among Dragons. The spiritual world and the unexplained beckons to them.

Like an aggravated, angry Dragon in literature and folklore, the people of this sign, if wronged, respond with quick tempers, egotistical demands, and are potentially self-destructive. They can be judgmental, belligerent, and stubborn.

Self-interest and self-indulgence can make them unfaithful in love, but only after they have won over their beloved with intense passion and dramatic conquest. Possessiveness is often a threat to their relationships. The Dragon thrives on competitiveness in all walks of life and this can be of particular concern in romantic partnerships.

As children they are typically loud and willful, and as parents, they can be authoritative and stern, but encouraging of independence in their offspring. The "warm" side of the Dragon parent is emotional generosity and compassion.

The Dragon never shies from responsibility, gives orders naturally, and easily gains the respect of employees and colleagues alike. The Dragon's energy and outsized confidence can be intimating to some yet most who come into contact with Dragon people admire and are inspired by their talents and abilities.

Auspicious careers: trial lawyer, priest, doctor, community organizer

YEAR OF THE DRAGON

ELEMENT
Yang Earth

SEASON
Spring

MONTH
April

HOUR
07:00–09:00

FENG SHUI DIRECTION
East Southeast

RANK
Fifth

WESTERN SIGN
Aries

FRAGRANCE
Tea Rose

FLOWER
Sweet Pea

FAMOUS DRAGONS

Sigmund Freud

Salvadore Dali

Sandra Bullock

Mae West

Marlene Dietrich

YEAR OF THE DRAGON

Compatability of the Dragon with the other zodiac signs:

Dragon and Rat–Socially compatible; both signs hold their own with an audience and both feed off of the other's energy. They do not stand in each other's way.

Dragon and Ox–Attractively opposite; the enthusiastic, charismatic Dragon wows the dependable, strong-willed Ox until the two wills clash. Finding a happy compromise is essential for a long-term relationship.

Dragon and Tiger–Passionately unpredictable; with two signs so characterized by extreme energy and enthusiasm for living, the possibilities are endless. High spirits and strong opinions will inevitably cause disagreements, but the joy of sharing life's journey will prevail.

Dragon and Rabbit–Sensitively syncopated; the give and take between these two signs helps maintain harmony between them. The extroverted, confident Dragon can threaten the mild-mannered Rabbit's sense of security.

Dragon and Dragon–Spontaneously combustible; this combination produces a fiery force in the most positive of ways! The Dragon duo attracts many admirers and quite rightly too. Their charm, vivacity, and interest in others keep friends coming back for more.

Dragon and Snake–Innately wise; the Dragon and the Snake recognize and admire the courage of the other, which gives them the insight into finding mutual ground.

YEAR OF THE DRAGON

Dragon and Horse—Practically turbulent; these signs share a zest for the exciting things in life, but when life inevitably turns on the mundane the relationship can hit the skids.

Dragon and Goat—Dissimilarly paced; the dreamy Goat and the assertive Dragon march to the beat of different drummers. They each admire the other's talents, however, and can give their friend or partner the ear and encouragement they seek.

Dragon and Monkey—Ideally attracted; two powerhouses combine when the Dragon and the Monkey form a relationship. Neither is daunted by the shine of the other. They are well balanced emotionally and mutually supportive.

Dragon and Rooster—Seriously fun; these two signs know how to enjoy life, but each has a serious side, which brings gravitas to the more important decisions they must make.

Dragon and Dog—Questionably apt; the skeptical Dog can be lambasted by the exuberant Dragon, growing increasingly annoyed with the Dragon's constant action which can generate arguments.

Dragon and Pig—Charmingly affectionate; the happy Pig welcomes the flair of the Dragon and accepts it with aplomb. They both love social gatherings. A deep understanding of the other makes for two really true friends or partners.

YEAR OF THE SNAKE

04 February 1905–24 January 1906	Wood Snake
23 January 1917–10 February 1918	Fire Snake
10 February 1929–29 January 1930	Earth Snake
27 January 1941–14 February 1942	Metal Snake
14 February 1953–02 February 1954	Water Snake
02 February 1965–20 January 1966	Wood Snake
18 February 1977–06 February 1978	Fire Snake
06 February 1989–26 January 1990	Earth Snake
24 January 2001–11 February 2002	Metal Snake
10 February 2013–30 January 2014	Water Snake
29 January 2025–16 February 2026	Wood Snake

As the saying goes, "The snake speaks with forked tongue," so Snake people are frequently smooth talkers who use this ability to their advantage in professional and personal relationships. They are naturally charming and exploit this trait to great success in business.

The Snake's destiny can be seen as achieving great things while operating from "backstage." That doesn't mean the Snake doesn't bring great force to bear on the issue at hand though. A sense of great timing, i.e., when to finally appear on stage, combined with patience, accumulated energy, and silent power give the Snake an undeniable ability to strike with unusually deft aim and hit its mark.

This trait can give Snake people, who above all desire their privacy, an air of mystery or secretiveness. In acting behind the scenes, the Snake is merely attempting to control the environment around her, not leaving life to chance. Order and planning is crucial to the Snake's well-being. Nevertheless, feelings rather than logic guide the decisions of the Snake.

YEAR OF THE SNAKE

Much time is spent in contemplation and thus the Snake typically has an opinion—his or her own—and has no need for others' advice. Esoteric and exotic styles are appealing to them.

Most Snakes select their friends very carefully and are attracted to those who, like themselves, think deeply and seriously. Spending as much time as they do in philosophical and intellectual musings, Snake people may with time develop psychic ability.

The solitary, self-reflecting side of a Snake if taken to extreme can result in self-indulgent and dishonest behavior. Possessiveness, procrastination, laziness, and generally odd behavior also at times can characterize Snakes.

Snake people are often facile in languages, mastering several in their lifetimes.

In love, Snakes are seductive and determined. Even if their eye wanders, one eye is still firmly on the current partner's comings and goings. Possessiveness can rear its ugly head. But when the Snake is content, the Snake's partner is the beneficiary of a playful and attentive soulmate.

Typical of his solitary, behind-the-scenes nature, the Snake's most popular and successful career paths are ones in which the Snake works independently. Articulate and often glib the Snake excels in the law, politics, and public relations. Reflection and contemplation, common traits of Snake people, help make Snakes insightful psychologists and astrologers.

Auspicious careers: lawyer, publicist, psychologist, astrologer

ELEMENT
Yin Fire

SEASON
Summer

MONTH
May

HOUR
09:00–11:00

FENG SHUI DIRECTION
South Southeast

RANK
Sixth

WESTERN SIGN
Taurus

FRAGRANCE
Musk

FLOWER
Lily of the Valley

FAMOUS SNAKES

Jacqueline Kennedy Onassis

Franklin Delano Roosevelt

Grace Kelly Rainier

Abraham Lincoln

John Malkovich

Greta Garbo

YEAR OF THE SNAKE

Compatability of the Snake with the other zodiac signs:

Snake and Rat–Keenly attuned; passion abounds between these two signs. The Snake is easily tempted by the fruit of another, of course, and if the Rat gets wind of an indiscretion, the Rat's insecurity bubbles up making it difficult to salvage the once exuberant emotional ties.

Snake and Ox–Positively partners; a deep karmic understanding exists between these two signs. The charming Snake is happy to venture into the world to make the couple's fortune and the steadfast Ox is content to keep the home fires burning.

Snake and Tiger–Irritatingly antagonistic; if ever two signs approach life in different ways, it's these two. The Tiger is action incarnate, while the Snake prefers strategy and analysis. Whether in matters of finance, romance or simply making dinner, if the two signs compromise and negotiate, they can be very happy.

Snake and Rabbit–Simply contemplative; the Rabbit and the Snake share the love of a quiet escape and privacy at home. Their evasion of the hectic world is often in search of beauty: natural as in the outdoors or the genious of man as in a museum or gallery.

Snake and Dragon–Innately wise; the Dragon and the Snake recognize and admire the courage of the other, which gives them the insight into finding mutual ground.

Snake and Snake–Closely attuned; charming and strategic, two Snakes make a magnetic couple. Shared goals, humor, and determination help this duo meet the challenges of life and a relationship if care is taken not to smother the other.

YEAR OF THE SNAKE

Snake and Horse–Deftly managed; both signs need space to roam and pursue their respective interests. Each understands what motivates the other and acts on this understanding to keep harmony in the relationship.

Snake and Goat–Nonroutinely committed; this pair loves the unusual and strains under the pressure of mundane deadlines.

Snake and Monkey–Opportunistically compatible; these two signs are not always in sync in terms of their perspective on life, but they do share high energy and creativity. When they act together and can adapt to the other's viewpoint, this combination can go far.

Snake and Rooster–Naturally empathetic; this couple shares an openness and honesty that helps build a strong bond and lasting relationship. The outward elegance of this pair is mirrored in their deepest feelings for the other.

Snake and Dog–Tenderly reassuring; the worldly wise Snake brings much stability and confidence to its relationship with the trusting Dog. The Dog appreciates the cleverness and independence of the Snake, rewarding friend or partner with loyalty and protection.

Snake and Pig–Understandingly independent; the affectionate is obvious in this pairing, but both signs require a certain amount of time to pursue solitary interests.

YEAR OF THE HORSE

25 January 1906–12 February 1907	Fire Horse
11 February 1918–31 January 1919	Earth Horse
30 January 1930–16 February 1931	Metal Horse
15 February 1942–04 February 1943	Water Horse
03 February 1954–23 February 1955	Wood Horse
21 January 1966–08 February 1967	Fire Horse
07 February 1978–27 January 1979	Earth Horse
27 January 1990–14 February 1991	Metal Horse
12 February 2002–31 January 2003	Water Horse
31 January 2014–18 February 2015	Wood Horse
17 February 2026–05 February 2027	Fire Horse

Horse people are high-spirited, lively, and full of energy. Like the horse that symbolizes them, they are usually amiable and easy-going and generally quite popular with a broad range of people. Everyone enjoys the Horse's company and the Horse thrills at being the center of attention. With a shake of a shiny mane and tail, the horse can quickly grab the crowd's attention, and in a similar manner the Horse steps into the limelight usually with great style and wearing snappy attire accented by a welcoming smile.

The Horse is quick-witted and cunning, yet many Horses lack confidence. A sharp mind, however, allows the Horse to anticipate and deflect the roadblocks that she will inevitably encounter.

Just as the horse is born to a life of racing or travel, many Horse people leave home young. Typically, Horse people, regardless of whether they stay or leave home, are good workers (just like the reliable work horse) and can deal well with money and finances. But with a flick of the head, the Horse can change course; many a Horse suffers from a short attention span. Although they are ambitious, Horses are rebellious and this trait can hinder the achievement of their goals.

The other side of the Horse's personality is a hot-blooded and hot-headed stallion who focuses mostly on self, but because the Horse works so determinedly, his efforts benefit the greater good. The Horse reaps the rewards of power, wealth, and respect as a result of his ability to get the job done.

Contradictions abound in the character of the Horse. The Horse can be sweet-natured yet arrogant, conceited yet humble, vivacious yet disinterested.

Movement is paramount to Horse people, therefore freedom and independence are essential elements for all Horses to be happy. They constantly seek new entertainment, often act spontaneously, and are viewed by many as unpredictable, prone to rapid mood changes although generally they do not suffer a fiery temper.

Horses approach life enthusiastically. With a facile and incisive mind, they are quick decision makers. New business ventures are often the result of a hunch or inspired insight. Many enjoy a very dependable sixth sense.

All their lives, Horses tend to get involved in numerous extracurricular activities. They have a grand talent for innovation. Because of a sharp wit, the Horse is above all capable of being a very successful politician with a strong ability to persuade a skeptical audience. She does not excel in any career that requires solitude or meditation because the Horse is an extrovert who performs best with strong, continued support from friends and family who love and admire her.

Auspicious careers: politician, entrepreneur, lawyer, diplomat

YEAR OF THE HORSE

ELEMENT
Yang Fire

SEASON
Summer

MONTH
June

HOUR
11:00–13:00

FENG SHUI DIRECTION
South

RANK
Seventh

WESTERN SIGN
Gemini

FRAGRANCE
Cedar

FLOWER
Rose

FAMOUS HORSES

Billy Graham

Neil Armstrong

Barbra Streisand

Cindy Crawford

Ulysses S. Grant

Sean Connery

YEAR OF THE HORSE

Compatability of the Horse with the other zodiac signs:

Horse and Rat–Emotionally charged; the Horse canters wildly through the fields of romance triggering the Rat's innate wariness to go to ground. The Horse can suffer the critical eye of the Rat, severing their previously uninhibited relationship.

Horse and Ox–Poorly suited; these two four-hooved signs march to different drummers. Restless and flighty, the Horse bounds away to discover new adventures, while the Ox, patient and supporting, watches in disappointment.

Horse and Tiger–Enthusiastically social; a shared passion for life and the people in it bind these two signs together. A very hectic social calendar makes for a chaotic home life.

Horse and Rabbit–Confidently devoted; romance truly blossoms between these two signs. The Horse's unbridled joy in showing love and tenderness to the Rabbit reassures the Rabbit of the Horse's devotion.

Horse and Dragon–Practically turbulent; these signs share a zest for the exciting things in life, but when life inevitably turns on the mundane the relationship can hit the skids.

Horse and Snake–Deftly managed; both signs need space to roam and pursue their respective interests. Each understands what motivates the other and acts on this understanding to keep harmony in the relationship.

YEAR OF THE HORSE

Horse and Horse–Quickly paced; two Horses make for a high-energy relationship. The Horse needs to be admired and stroked, so when or if this crucial element is neglected the search for greener pastures is sure to ensue.

Horse and Goat–Pleasantly unpredictable; the Horse leads the Goat in search of new adventures and the joint exploits keep the relationship lively and interesting for both signs.

Horse and Monkey–Carefully maneuvered; this combination requires a joint effort to get the kinks out. Cautious, hesitant Monkey shies away from emotionally open Horse, but if the Horse can demonstrate that her emotions are genuine, the Monkey will gradually feel more confident in the relationship.

Horse and Rooster–Competitively challenged; both the Horse and the Rooster can place undue importance on the superficial and the need to prevail. An effort to search for deeper meaning will help the relationship grow.

Horse and Dog–Practically protective; the Horse is a wanderer for whom the Dog is content to wait. The Horse benefits from the practical support of the Dog, but should be careful not to take advantage of the Dog's loyal nature.

Horse and Pig–Expressly romantic; these two signs enjoy the romance in life and sharing new experiences. The Horse can run ahead of the Pig, circling back when he needs attention and affection. From time to time, however, this may cause resentment in the patient Pig.

YEAR OF THE GOAT

13 February 1907–01 February 1908	Fire Goat
01 February 1919–19 February 1920	Earth Goat
17 February 1931–05 February 1932	Metal Goat
05 February 1943–24 January 1944	Water Goat
24 January 1955–11 February 1956	Wood Goat
09 February 1967–29 January 1968	Fire Goat
28 January 1979–15 February 1980	Earth Goat
15 February 1991–03 February 1992	Metal Goat
01 February 2003–21 January 2004	Water Goat
19 February 2015–07 February 2016	Wood Goat
06 February 2027–25 January 2028	Fire Goat

Goat people are elegant and artistic, but also often shy and pessimistic. Religion and spirituality usually play a large role in their lives. Not always the most articulate of the zodiac signs, Goats are nevertheless passionate about what they do and what they believe in. As a result, they generally do not have to worry about money and can enjoy the finer things in life.

Goats are known for impulsive outbursts that can offend others. Their charm makes up for the majority of slights, however. In addition to being charming and witty, they are wise, gentle, compassionate, and forgive easily. Goats are the good Samaritans of the Chinese zodiac.

Ironically, Goats are easily hurt if they are criticized. Turn about is not fair play! Like the goat that is their sign, Goat people enjoy a good wander and do not tolerate much discipline. It is difficult for them to work under pressure and need to do things at their own speed. A spouse or business partner usually is responsible for keeping their Goat on task in order to utilize their talents.

YEAR OF THE GOAT

Goats tend to hold their feelings close to the vest. Only with great reticence do they come clean with what they are thinking or what is bothering them. They worry about all and sundry and depend on their friends and family to cheer them up and assuage their concerns.

Goats are devoted to their family and always remember everyone's birthday. They hate for anyone to be displeased with them, especially those they love and trust. It is hard for them to deal directly with an unpleasant issue and they will generally beat around the bush until the other party demands a true accounting of their feelings. Goats are extremely sensitive and often overreact. They need reassurance to maintain a happy and contented emotional state.

Overspending is a definite problem for Goat people although money seems to flow into their hands in sufficient amounts to pay for what they buy. Being practical is a real challenge for them. They love luxurious surroundings and material possessions. An unattractive environment will depress Goats.

Creative fields in which they can freely pursue their interests and can work unhindered by constraints are attractive to many Goats. Even as a child, the imaginative Goat is drawn to artistic expression, so parents of Goat children would do well to encourage their little kid to explore his or her talents and creative musings.

In general, Goats are adaptable, but are known for occasional moodiness and pouting when they are brooding about a perceived wrong. Love, attention, and approval are what is needed for them to recover their good nature.

Auspicious careers: doctor, artist, actor, scientist, geologist

YEAR OF THE GOAT

ELEMENT
Yin Earth

SEASON
Summer

MONTH
July

HOUR
13:00–15:00

FENG SHUI DIRECTION
South Southwest

RANK
Eighth

WESTERN SIGN
Cancer

FRAGRANCE
Orange Bergamot

FLOWER
Larkspur

FAMOUS GOATS

Michelangelo

John Kerry

Goldie Hawn

Barbara Walters

Franz Liszt

Mark Twain

YEAR OF THE GOAT

Compatability of the Goat with the other zodiac signs:

Goat and Rat–Determinedly different; these two signs must find common ground to build a friendship or partnership. The Rat forges ahead while the Goat hangs back to chew his cud.

Goat and Ox–Decidedly dissimilar; opposite approaches to life mean unbridled consternation in partnership. Sensible, organized Ox does not see eye to eye with fanciful Goat, but Goat's good intentions can melt away Ox's distain.

Goat and Tiger–Reassuringly protective; the Tiger is eager to guard the Goat against unwanted confrontations and demands. Both signs are independent in their own ways and neither wishes to feel trapped in a relationship.

Goat and Rabbit–Truly matched; the world is their oyster and these two signs explore it with abandon! When one is anxious, the other is a calming influence, and vice versa, allowing them to proceed unabated with their adventures.

Goat and Dragon–Dissimilarly paced; the dreamy Goat and the assertive Dragon march to the beat of different drummers. They each admire the other's talents, however, and can give the their friend or partner the ear and encouragement they seek.

Goat and Snake–Nonroutinely committed; this pair loves the unusual and strains under the pressure of mundane deadlines.

YEAR OF THE GOAT

Goat and Horse–Pleasantly unpredictable; the Horse leads the Goat in search of new adventures and the joint exploits keep the relationship lively and interesting for both signs.

Goat and Goat–Spiritually attuned; two Goats share an affinity for the realm beyond the practical realities of earthly living, but alas the mundane and routine are necessary so divvy up the tasks and get on with it!

Goat and Monkey–Constructively indulgent; the Goat and the Monkey indulge each other with travel and nights on the town, but clever Monkey keeps a watchful eye on career, finances, and deadlines, which less confident Goat truly appreciates.

Goat and Rooster–Potentially ill-suited; these two signs exhibit too much push-and-pull to be happy every after. Independent Goat may be too busy wandering to notice that high-flying Rooster really needs reasurrance and affirmation.

Goat and Dog–Insufficiently optimistic; both the Goat and the Dog have periods of anxiety and worry that can stress their relationship. Working to be more overtly optimistic can help allay problems. A true fondness for each other can also mend broken fences.

Goat and Pig–Appreciatively sensitive; the Goat and the Pig understand each other's need to roam. Sensible Pig can artfully advise creative Goat without giving offense.

YEAR OF THE MONKEY

02 February 1908–21 January 1909	Earth Monkey
20 February 1920–07 February 1921	Metal Monkey
06 February 1932–25 January 1933	Water Monkey
25 January 1944–12 February 1945	Wood Monkey
12 February 1956–30 January 1957	Fire Monkey
30 January 1968–16 February 1969	Earth Monkey
16 February 1980–04 February 1981	Metal Monkey
04 February 1992–22 January 1993	Water Monkey
22 January 2004–08 February 2005	Wood Monkey
08 February 2016–27 January 2017	Fire Monkey
26 January 2028–12 February 2029	Earth Monkey

Monkeys are fun-loving people who are always cheerful and energetic. They are also quite clever, talented, creative, and generous.

Monkey people are typically the center of attention at most functions. Charm and a humorous view of life are a large reason for their popularity. They are diplomatic, hiding their true opinions of others when it is best to do so, typically beneath outward gregariousness. But they wear their emotions on their sleeve.

Like Curious George, Monkey people are continually inquiring and interested in learning new things. They are very good at problem solving and are therefore quite successful in business. Their opportunism and keen competitive instinct join together to produce an employee or business leader who can capture a market and rapidly turn a profit. Cunning and rather wily, they are sometimes self-centered, operating to their own benefit. They have the ability to persuade themselves and everyone around them that they are in the right.

YEAR OF THE MONKEY

Regardless of the career a Monkey chooses, his or her wit and good fortune will bring success. Monkey-born people have a compelling need to be noticed, which leads to careers in show business, politics, diplomacy, and even in industry, where they can rise to the top of the pyramid. Publicity is their friend—at least that's how they see it—and they can behave in an audacious manner with little regard for their reputation in order to stay in the public eye.

The Monkey is talkative, a good conversationalist, and attracts a broad array of friends. Monkeys are rarely bored, mainly because they seek continual stimulation to keep themselves amused. Sometimes, Monkey's cleverness can become mettlesome and manipulative. They possess an insightfulness into others' characters that they are able to use to their advantage.

Highly adaptable and versatile, the Monkey is enthusiastic about every aspect of life and is especially fascinated by art: its refinement, originality, and luxury. Monkeys can quickly assimilate facts and figures, picking up new skills and techniques almost instantaneously.

As friends, Monkeys are loyal and devoted. As spouses, they are passionate, but can tire of the relationship all too soon. They look for the same qualities in their partners that they exhibit themselves: cleverness, gregariousness, and intelligence. Ultimately, the goal is to have others in their life who can stimulate them intellectually as well as emotionally.

Monkeys adore the thrill of the new, so he or she is rather fickle in romance. A critical nature as well as good intuition can mean that ardor is cooled quickly if the romantic combination is not propitious. A good sense of humor usually comes to the rescue.

Auspicious careers: entrepreneur, comedian, airline pilot, travel agent

YEAR OF THE MONKEY

ELEMENT
Yang Metal

SEASON
Autumn

MONTH
August

HOUR
15:00–17:00

FENG SHUI DIRECTION
West Southwest

RANK
Ninth

WESTERN SIGN
Leo

FRAGRANCE
Ylang Ylang

FLOWER
Poppy

FAMOUS MONKEYS

Buster Keaton

Annie Oakley

Danny DeVito

Harry Houdini

Elizabeth Taylor

Susan B. Anthony

YEAR OF THE MONKEY

Compatability of the Monkey with the other zodiac signs:

Monkey and Rat–Highly competitive; the intellectual and sensual high-wire act of the Monkey is not to be outdone by the overwhelming intensity and passion of the Rat. But when the two energies collide, one or both suffers the fall.

Monkey and Ox–Slowly trusting; with time these two signs gradually learn to appreciate the other's traits that balance their own. Chattering Monkey stays busy, only to return home to responsible Ox. Nevertheless, Ox can grow tired of Monkey's vivacity and gregariousness.

Monkey and Tiger–Energetically adventurous; both the Tiger and the Monkey literally jump at any new opportunity for exploration and new experiences, but the Monkey thinks before jumping and is usually the one to resolve obstacles.

Monkey and Rabbit–Emotionally intuitive; the clever Monkey's schemes are kept in check by the observant, caring Rabbit who gently guides them both toward a mutual understanding that allows them to grow and learn together.

Monkey and Dragon–Ideally attracted; two powerhouses combine when the Dragon and the Monkey form a relationship. Neither is daunted by the shine of the other. They are well balanced emotionally and mutually supportive.

Monkey and Snake–Opportunistically compatible; these two signs are not always in sync in terms of their perspective on life, but they do share high energy and creativity. When they act together and can adapt to the other's viewpoint, this combination can go far.

YEAR OF THE MONKEY

Monkey and Horse—Carefully maneuvered; this combination requires a joint effort to get the kinks out. Cautious, hesitant Monkey shies away from emotionally open Horse, but if the Horse can demonstrate that her emotions are genuine, the Monkey will gradually feel more confident in the relationship.

Monkey and Goat—Constructively indulgent; the Goat and the Monkey indulge each other with travel and nights on the town, but clever Monkey keeps a watchful eye on career, finances, and deadlines, which less confident Goat truly appreciates.

Monkey and Monkey—Happily captivated; two charming Monkeys play games with the other but willfully acknowledge that they are laying the groundwork for a stimulating life together. They shy away from overt emotional displays, but that belies the depth of their feelings.

Monkey and Rooster—Discerningly different; whereas the Rooster is a straight shooter, Monkey is downright cunning. Rooster is impulsive, while Monkey is analytical. Tolerance of each other's approaches to life is the ticket to a long and rewarding relationship.

Monkey and Dog—Predictably confounding; each of these signs is often puzzled by the other's behavior. Sensible Dog can be shocked by wily Monkey's antics.

Monkey and Pig—Subtly manipulative; these two signs are wise to the other's motivations. This pairing has fun together. Loyal Pig provides gregarious Monkey comfort and support.

YEAR OF THE ROOSTER

26 January 1897–11 February 1898	Fire Rooster
22 January 1909–09 February 1910	Earth Rooster
08 February 1921–27 January 1922	Metal Rooster
26 January 1933–13 February 1934	Water Rooster
13 February 1945–01 February 1946	Wood Rooster
31 January 1957–17 February 1958	Fire Rooster
17 February 1969–05 February 1970	Earth Rooster
05 February 1981–24 January 1982	Metal Rooster
23 January 1993–09 February 1994	Water Rooster
09 February 2005–28 January 2006	Wood Rooster
28 January 2017–15 February 2018	Fire Rooster
13 February 2029–02 February 2030	Earth Rooster

Roosters are self-assured with personalities that dominate in many situations. They are hardworking, resourceful, and talented. Around others, they are vivacious, amusing, and popular. But like the cocky rooster of the farmyard, Roosters can be conceited, vain, and boastful.

Roosters enjoy being the center of attention and are often the life of the party. Rooster people are articulate, frank, and honest, but can be too blunt. The Rooster is a talented debater, can argue and support his or her opinions, and makes an excellent journalist or writer.

Organization makes Roosters tick. Keeping their affairs in order, accounts up to date, and documents alphabetically filed away is symbolic of the control they seek and need in life. They function best in an environment upon which routine and schedule are imposed. They enjoy working to deadlines.

YEAR OF THE ROOSTER

Before making a decision, Roosters carefully consider all sides of the situation. Their reflective and analytical abilities are used to constantly question and reaffirm their point of view, which only strengthens their conviction that their position is correct. Their opinions are not arrived at lightly.

Financial management is a reliable strength on both private and professional levels. In money matters, Roosters are prudent and vigilant, observant and precise. They are excellent managers of other people's money and make outstanding financial advisers, bank managers, and accountants. Because Rooster people are skeptical and cautious, they are not easily fooled.

Roosters see the world as either black or white and this applies to people as well. When they meet new people, they immediately love or hate them. Rooster people are above all honest and have no qualms in speaking their mind. This characteristic can really get them into hot water from time to time!

Appearance and style are important to Roosters and they work hard to always look their best–not only for themselves but also to attract attention and admiration.

Their romantic lives are filled with excitement and tumult. To the outside eye, they may appear to dominate their partner, but this is typically just part of the game–making sparks fly!–that the two play privately. Reality is a much more balanced give and take. Because of their unremitting honesty, when in a permanent relationship, Roosters are highly unlikely to deceive or cheat on their partners.

Auspicious careers: economist, writer, journalist, accountant, financial advisor, detective, psychiatrist

ELEMENT
Yin Metal

SEASON
Autumn

MONTH
September

HOUR
17:00–19:00

FENG SHUI DIRECTION
West

RANK
Tenth

WESTERN SIGN
Virgo

FRAGRANCE
Gardenia

FLOWER
Aster

FAMOUS ROOSTERS

Catherine the Great

Rudyard Kipling

Prince Philip

Nancy Reagan

Steve Martin

Debra Kerr

YEAR OF THE ROOSTER

Compatability of the Rooster with the other zodiac signs:

Rooster and Rat–Initially at odds; opposites attract but it make take some time before these two signs recognize their winning combination. At first, in the Rat's eyes the Rooster may appear superficial and frivolous, but perseverence tells the tale. The Rooster's courage and analytical nature will win over the critical Rat.

Rooster and Ox–Delightfully happy; the perfect blend of fun and respect weaves the fabric of a long-lasting relationship. The Rooster brings the color and design whereas the Ox brings the patience and tenacity. Stay clear of the sparks these two generate!

Rooster and Tiger–Critically frank; neither sign hesitates to speak its mind. Be patient with the other's censure and be honest about your own feelings.

Rooster and Rabbit–Energetically unbalanced; this is a difficult pairing if emotional equilibrium is the goal. The Rabbit craves harmony and predictability, while the Rooster lives for action and adventure.

Rooster and Dragon–Seriously fun; these two signs know how to enjoy life, but each has a serious side, which brings gravitas to the more important decisions they must make.

Rooster and Snake–Naturally empathetic; this couple shares an openness and honesty that helps build a strong bond and lasting relationship. The outward elegance of this pair is mirrored in their deepest feelings for the other.

Rooster and Horse—Competitively challenged; both the Horse and the Rooster can place undue importance on the superficial and the need to prevail. An effort to search for deeper meaning will help the relationship grow.

Rooster and Goat—Potentially ill-suited; these two signs exhibit too much push-and-pull to be happy every after. Independent Goat may be too busy wandering to notice that high-flying Rooster really needs reasurrance and affirmation.

Rooster and Monkey—Discerningly different; whereas the Rooster is a straight shooter, Monkey is downright cunning. Rooster is impulsive, while Monkey is analytical. Tolerance of each other's approaches to life is the ticket to a long and rewarding relationship.

Rooster and Rooster—Critically admiring; no holes are barred in this duo's relationship. Each speaks his or her mind, which can sometimes be hurtful, but their approval and appreciation of the other's liveliness, courage, and confidence wins the day.

Rooster and Dog—Thoughtfully resilient; both of these signs have a deeper, reflective side and connect on that level. The Rooster is more independent and outspoken than the Dog, but the Dog is insightful enough to appreciate the Rooster's genuine interest in his well being.

Rooster and Pig—Clearly companionable; the low-key Pig is content to bask in the light that burns brightly around the Rooster because the Pig can also see the light that burns brightly inside the Rooster's soul.

YEAR OF THE DOG

22 January 1898–09 February 1899	Earth Dog
10 February 1910–29 January 1911	Metal Dog
28 January 1922–15 February 1923	Water Dog
14 February 1934–03 February 1935	Wood Dog
02 February 1946–21 January 1947	Fire Dog
18 February 1958–07 February 1959	Earth Dog
06 February 1970–26 January 1971	Metal Dog
25 January 1982–12 February 1983	Water Dog
10 February 1994–30 January 1995	Wood Dog
29 January 2006–17 February 2007	Fire Dog
16 February 2018–04 February 2019	Earth Dog
03 February 2030–22 January 2031	Metal Dog

Dog people are humanitarians. They are energized by the act of giving and are willing to sacrifice their own dreams, ambitions, and desires for others, especially those they love. They are viewed as the least materialistic of all the signs in the Chinese zodiac.

Intensely loyal to those they care about, Dogs will quickly defend any family member or friend who is being attacked verbally or physically. Not surprisingly, they are known for championing the underdog.

On a quest to bring equilibrium to a tumultuous world, Dogs speak out loudly against injustice and wrongdoing and willingly take action to improve others' circumstances. Their warmth, empathy, and genuine interest in others mean that they always have a network of numerous close friends. They are always willing to do whatever it takes to help others, even to the point of self-sacrifice.

YEAR OF THE DOG

The Dog makes a faithful, honest, and steadfast friend who liberally gives advice to those around her. Whereas Dogs can be generous and warm-hearted, they can also be guarded and defensive. Because they truly believe they know best, they often appear to be a know-it-all and can be quite stubborn in their opinions.

Dogs accomplish goals quickly because they never really relax; they are ever vigilant and active in their heart and mind because of an underlying sense of uncertainty. Most Dogs are reluctant to experience change in their lives, and it is forced upon them with only grudging acceptance.

The Dog tends to repress his feelings until he believes it is absolutely necessary to expose them. He is plagued with a generally pessimistic view of his own life and can be nostalgic about the past.

Due to an altruistic nature and high moral integrity, Dog people often fill important roles in society. They are typically highly regarded and trusted by all those who deal with them. Influential people tend to support them, which is helpful to their career prospects. The Dog's ideas will be profound and original. No other sign unites decency, goodness, and passion for accomplishment associated with such little personal ambition.

Dogs do not give their affections quickly or impulsively, but when they do, the friendships they establish are for life. In romance, Dogs gives the impression of being aloof, but this is misleading. More often than not they are simply anxious and unsure of their own feelings. Personal relationships are critical to the Dog's happiness, much more so than material possessions, financial resources, or career success. In love, the most important characteristic of Dogs is their loyalty and they will stick to their partners forever.

Auspicious careers: entrepreneur, priest, educator

YEAR OF THE DOG

ELEMENT
Yang Earth

SEASON
Autumn

MONTH
October

HOUR
19:00–21:00

FENG SHUI DIRECTION
West Northwest

RANK
Eleventh

WESTERN SIGN
Libra

FRAGRANCE
Balsam

FLOWER
Orange Blossom

FAMOUS DOGS

Claudia Schiffer

Victor Hugo

Golda Meir

Jamie Lee Curtis

Brigitte Bardot

Winston Churchill

YEAR OF THE DOG

Compatability of the Dog with the other zodiac signs:

Dog and Rat–Fearlessly supportive; trustworthy Dog and watchful Rat can forge a life-long bond.

Dog and Ox–Unerring fealty; the loyal natures of both signs seal their hearts and minds for the long haul. Fretting Dog is soothed by reliable Ox enabling the partners to meet life's challenges head on, even in times of pain and sorrow.

Dog and Tiger–Keenly compassionate; these signs work well together to fight for those less fortunate.

Dog and Rabbit–Sensibly realistic; the traits of honor and reliability are shared by these two signs. Both see the world and their place in it the same way, and together can guard against most eventualities that threaten them.

Dog and Dragon–Questionably apt; the skeptical Dog can be lambasted by the exuberant Dragon, growing increasingly annoyed with the Dragon's constant action which can generate arguments.

Dog and Snake–Tenderly reassuring; the worldly wise Snake brings much stability and confidence to its relationship with the trusting Dog. The Dog appreciates the cleverness and independence of the Snake, rewarding friend or partner with loyalty and protection.

YEAR OF THE DOG

Dog and Horse–Practically protective; the Horse is a wanderer for whom the Dog is content to wait. The Horse benefits from the practical support of the Dog, but should be careful not to take advantage of the Dog's loyal nature.

Dog and Goat–Insufficiently optimistic; both the Goat and the Dog have periods of anxiety and worry that can stress their relationship. Working to be more overtly optimistic can help allay problems. A true fondness for each other can also mend broken fences.

Dog and Monkey–Predictably confounding; each of these signs is often puzzled by the other's behavior. Sensible Dog can be shocked by wily Monkey's antics.

Dog and Rooster–Thoughtfully resilient; both of these signs have a deeper, reflective side and connect on that level. The Rooster is more independent and outspoken than the Dog, but the Dog is insightful enough to appreciate the Rooster's genuine interest in his well being.

Dog and Dog–Courageously committed; two of a kind, these signs are happiest when dedicated to building a safe, secure joint venture. They give each other strength and comfort when times are rocky and they seek constancy and calm in all aspects of their relationship.

Dog and Pig–Nicely nuanced; fun-loving Pig can soothe suspicious, moody Dog who is always willing to offer loyalty and protection to the sometimes naive Pig.

YEAR OF THE PIG

10 February 1889–30 January 1900	Earth Pig
30 January 1911–17 February 1912	Metal Pig
16 February 1923–04 February 1924	Water Pig
04 February 1935–23 January 1936	Wood Pig
22 January 1947–09 February 1948	Fire Pig
08 February 1959–27 January 1960	Earth Pig
27 January 1971–14 February 1972	Metal Pig
13 February 1983–01 February 1984	Water Pig
31 January 1995–18 February 1996	Wood Pig
18 February 2007–06 February 2008	Fire Pig
05 February 2019–24 January 2020	Earth Pig
23 January 2031–10 February 2032	Metal Pig

Sincerity and virtue are traits found in most Pig people. The Pig feels guilty for the slightest error and is very indulgent and forgiving of others. She does not suffer deceit or pretense and dislikes being the center of attention. On the one hand, the Pig is magnanimous, gallant, and trustworthy, but on the other hand he is naive, insecure, and vulnerable and so can be duped easily. Fortunately, the Pig accepts his own faults and those of others with enduring forbearance.

The Pig is so sincere and honest – a veritable straight shooter - that she can be fooled easily by the bad faith of others; the Pig believes unquestionably what she is told by others.

People born in the Year of the Pig crave luxury in their surroundings, their clothes, their food and drink. Therefore, they can be extravagant. They enjoy pampering themselves and those they love and are absolutely sensual in the true sense of the word: all five senses (vision, hearing, smell, taste, and touch) must be pleased. The indulgences they allow themselves can sometimes verge on gluttony.

YEAR OF THE PIG

Pigs make wonderfully fun and lively companions. They are cheerful and love social occasions. Typically, the Pig is quietly compatible with the group and can be viewed as reserved and aloof, but when the Pig becomes attuned to his surroundings and comfortable with the people around him, nothing can stop his personality from profusely bubbling out for the remainder of the evening.

Although the Pig reads insatiably, he reads anything he finds at hand. He professes to be an intellectual, always on the hunt for more knowledge, whereas the reality is that his quest is more superficial than deep. Pigs often verge on laziness. Luck, however, protects them against most stumbling blocks. Pigs can be very practical and logical and exhibit great composure even under the most stressful of circumstances.

The Pig will do her duty and pursue her goals and ambitions with every ounce of strength and determination she can summon. Her strength emanates from her soul and is a force to be reckoned with. Before making a critical decision, Pigs will deliberate, ponder, and internally debate the issue, but once coming to a conclusion, nothing can cause the Pig to waiver. Observers may interpret the deliberating process as the Pig being indecisive, but in fact the Pig is merely being thorough.

Pigs do not shy away from work and will generally succeed in their careers, especially if they work independently. Affluence is important to them and fortunately money and career opportunities are abundant throughout their lives.

Like the pig that symbolizes them, Pig people can turn vicious if cornered. If their friendship and pleasant nature are abused, they will abruptly end the friendship. In love, Pigs wear their emotions on their sleeves and can be badly hurt if deceived by an uncaring, dishonest person. Friendship is the most valuable part of an intimate relationship for a Pig.

Auspicious careers: art dealer, attorney, researcher, poet, painter

YEAR OF THE PIG

ELEMENT
Yin Water

SEASON
Winter

MONTH
November

HOUR
21:00–23:00

FENG SHUI DIRECTION
North Northwest

RANK
Twelfth

WESTERN SIGN
Scorpio

FRAGRANCE
Floral

FLOWER
Chrysanthemum

FAMOUS PIGS

Farrah Fawcett

Steven Spielberg

Henry Ford

Arnold Schwarzenegger

Lucille Ball

Ralph Waldo Emerson

YEAR OF THE PIG

Compatability of the Pig with the other zodiac signs:

Pig and Rat–Happily affectionate; innocent and cheerful Pig takes Rat's demanding nature in stride. Pig's compassion assuages Rat's perception that she is misunderstood.

Pig and Ox–Soulfully suited; old-fashioned values keep these two cosily at home most nights, but when playful Pig persuades parsimonious Ox to spring for a night on the town, both appreciate the gift the other brings to their relationship.

Pig and Tiger–Unbounded friendship; balancing each sign's needs for companionship and freedom is the key to mutual happiness. The Pig listens to the advice of the Tiger, and the Tiger responds to the admonitions of the Pig.

Pig and Rabbit–Naturally harmonious; these signs find it very easy to be together, whether in conversation at home or on a hike through the forest. Listening to each other is the path to achieving their dreams.

Pig and Dragon–Charmingly affectionate; the happy Pig welcomes the flair of the Dragon and accepts it with aplomb. They both love social gatherings. A deep understanding of the other makes for two really true friends or partners.

Pig and Snake–Understandingly independent; the affectionate is obvious in this pairing, but both signs require a certain amount of time to pursue solitary interests.

YEAR OF THE PIG

Pig and Horse– Expressly romantic; these two signs enjoy the romance in life and sharing new experiences. The Horse can run ahead of the Pig, circling back when he needs attention and affection. From time to time, however, this may cause resentment in the patient Pig.

Pig and Goat–Appreciatively sensitive; the Goat and the Pig understand each other's need to roam. Sensible Pig can artfully advise creative Goat without giving offense.

Pig and Monkey–Subtly manipulative; these two signs are wise to the other's motivations. This pairing has fun together. Loyal Pig provides gregarious Monkey comfort and support.

Pig and Rooster–Clearly companionable; the low-key Pig is content to bask in the light that burns brightly around the Rooster because the Pig can also see the light that burns brightly inside the Rooster's soul.

Pig and Dog–Nicely nuanced; fun-loving Pig can soothe suspicious, moody Dog who is always willing to offer loyalty and protection to sometimes naive Pig.

Pig and Pig–Tempestuously affectionate; you two know each well and what exactly pushes the other's buttons. The two Pigs share a love of the open road, but also time spent in quiet contemplation at home. Neither holds a grudge for long.

ANIMAL TYPE

Year	Characteristics of Person Born in Year
Wood Rat, Rat on the Roof	Intelligent, impatient, may lack follow-through.
Fire Rat, Rat in the Field	Overwhelming energy, can be intolerant, undiplomatic.
Earth Rat, Rat in the Warehouse	Adaptable, trusting, sociable.
Metal Rat, Rat on the Beam	Good in crisis, realistic, born to organize.
Water Rat, Rat on the Mountain	Smiling outside, nervous inside, holds emotions close to the vest.
Wood Ox, Ox in the Sea	Charming, dependable, adventurous, large circle of friends.
Fire Ox, Ox in the Lake	Generous to a fault, empathetic to those less fortunate.
Earth Ox, Ox Inside the Gate	Sometimes outspoken, independent worker, candid nature.
Metal Ox, Ox on the Way	Analytical, good social skills, keen negotiator.
Water Ox, Ox Outside the Gate	Slow and steady, patience can actualize goals.
Wood Tiger, Tiger in the Forest	Knowledgeable, little patience for the irrelevant.
Fire Tiger, Tiger Crossing the Mountain	Emotional, easily rattled in the face of problems.
Earth Tiger, Tiger Descending the Mountain	Moody, but doesn't hold grudges, industrious.
Metal Tiger, Tiger Passing Through the Forest	Reflective, candid, duty-bound to be honest.
Water Tiger, Tiger Standing Still	Observant, analytical, determined, adaptable.

ANIMAL TYPE

Year	Characteristics of Person Born in Year
Wood Rabbit, Rabbit Looking at Moon	Optimistic, encouraging, dedicated to work, excitable.
Fire Rabbit, Rabbit Leaving Forest	Prefers to fit in, can be anxious about responsibility.
Earth Rabbit, Rabbit in Burrow	Outwardly carefree, inwardly less so but strong and courageous.
Metal Rabbit, Rabbit Running in the Forest	Lucky and happy, can turn lemons into lemonade.
Water Rabbit, Buddha Rabbit	Seeks justice and achievement, sensitive and organized.
Wood Dragon, Yielding Dragon	Distinctive presence, adaptable, thoughtful.
Fire Dragon, Angry Dragon	Confident in your many talents, charismatic.
Earth Dragon, Dragon in the Rain	Courageous, industrious, very resourceful.
Metal Dragon, Cheerful Dragon	Separates professional and personal life, strongly motivated by justice and right.
Water Dragon, Dragon Flying to Heaven	A bit of a nomad, energetic, seeks variety of life.
Wood Snake, Prosperous Snake	Good judge of character, diligent, caring personality.
Fire Snake, Snake Sleeping in Winter	Ambitious, intelligent, good financial sense.
Earth Snake, Snake in the Grass	Tends to overspend, sharp mind in business affairs.
Metal Snake, Snake Exiting Hole	Perhaps a late bloomer, honest, popular.
Water Snake, Snake in the Fish Pond	Dedicated, unconventional, determined.

ANIMAL TYPE

Year	Characteristics of Person Born in Year
Wood Horse, Horse in the Hall	Straight arrow, sometimes innocently tactless, loyal.
Fire Horse, Horse in the Army	Frugal, independent, hardworking, lively.
Earth Horse, Horse in the Clouds	Generous, compassionate, defender of the less fortunate.
Metal Horse, Horse on the Way	Inspirational leader, complicated personal relationships.
Water Horse, Horse Inside the Gate	Enthusiastically engage the new, empathetic, gentle.
Wood Goat, Prosperous Goat	Vulnerable, idealistic, lucky in friendship.
Fire Goat, Goat in Flock of Sheep	Supporter of worthy causes, outspoken, determined.
Earth Goat, Goat Respected by Others	Diligent worker, respected, tends to reach financial goals.
Metal Goat, Lonely Goat	Moody, truth seeker, easily influenced by world events.
Water Goat, Goat Running on the Mountain	Skilled debater, naturally elegant, kindly opinionated.
Wood Monkey, Elegant Monkey	Moody, seeks financial security, bargain hunter.
Fire Monkey, Monkey Climbing a Tree	Emotionally resolute, witty, good conversationalist.
Earth Monkey, Monkey Climbing the Mountain	Outstanding problem solver, rarely deceived by others.
Metal Monkey, Lonely Monkey	Impatient, but thoroughly dedicated worker, insightful.
Water Monkey, Monkey in a Fruit Tree	Takes time with appearance, active, sometimes impulsive.

ANIMAL TYPE

Year	Characteristics of Person Born in Year
Wood Rooster, Rooster in the Hen House	Good negotiator, enthusiastic zest for life, difficulty keeping secrets.
Fire Rooster, Singing Rooster	Sometimes unrealistically optimistic, opinionated.
Earth Rooster, Lonely Rooster	Lucky, cheerful, attracted to influential friends.
Metal Rooster, Rooster Announcing the Dawn	Financially fortunate, intuitive, impulsive in interactions.
Water Rooster, Rooster in a Cage	Driven, leader, strong debater, life-long learner.
Wood Dog, Dog on Guard	Tireless negotiator, stubborn, reflective.
Fire Dog, Sleepy Dog	Very relaxed nature, prefers to avoid decisions and deadlines.
Earth Dog, Dog Going into the Mountain	Intuitive, generous, independent, exercises good judgment.
Metal Dog, Temple Dog	Happily content, strong character, supports the downtrodden.
Water Dog, Family Dog	Fluctuating fortunes, supportive friends and family.
Wood Pig, Pig Passing By	Outspoken, honest, tends to be closer with friends than family.
Fire Pig, Pig Passing the Mountain	Loyal to personal commitments, faces challenges well.
Earth Pig, Monastery Pig	Intelligent, adaptable, optimistic, opportunistic.
Metal Pig, Pig in the Garden	Confident, independent, not nosey.
Water Pig, Pig in the Forest	Empathetic, purposeful, sometimes obstinate, as good as your word.

INDEX